ideals® CHRISTMAS

More Than 50 Years of Celebrating Life's Most Treasured Moments

Vol. 53, No. 8

"Ah! dearest Jesus, holy child,
Make Thee a bed, soft, undefiled,
Within my heart that it may be
A quiet chamber kept for Thee."

—Martin Luther

Country Chronicle
6

Featured Photograph
8

Traveler's Diary
10

Collector's Corner
16

Readers' Reflections
20

Remember When
24

Devotions from the Heart
28

Handmade Heirloom
32

Ideals' Family Recipes
36

My Favorite Memory
40

A Slice of Life
42

For the Children
46

Legendary Americans
64

Bits & Pieces
68

From My Garden Journal
70

Our Heritage
72

Through My Window
76

Readers' Forum
86

IDEALS—Vol. 53, No. 8 December MCMXCVI IDEALS (ISSN 0019-137X) is published eight times a year:
February, March, May, June, August, September, November, December by
IDEALS PUBLICATIONS INCORPORATED, 535 Metroplex Drive, Suite 250, Nashville, TN 37211.
Periodical postage paid at Nashville, Tennessee, and additional mailing offices.
Copyright © MCMXCVI by IDEALS PUBLICATIONS INCORPORATED.
POSTMASTER: Send address changes to Ideals, PO Box 305300, Nashville, TN 37230. All rights reserved.
Title IDEALS registered U.S. Patent Office.

SINGLE ISSUE—U.S. $5.95 USD; Higher in Canada
ONE-YEAR SUBSCRIPTION—U.S. $19.95 USD; Canada $36.00 CDN (incl. GST and shipping); Foreign $25.95 USD
TWO-YEAR SUBSCRIPTION—U.S. $35.95 USD; Canada $66.50 CDN (incl. GST and shipping); Foreign $47.95 USD

The cover and entire contents of IDEALS are fully protected by copyright and must not be reproduced in any manner whatsoever.

Printed and bound in USA by Quebecor Printing. Printed on Weyerhaeuser Husky.

The paper used in this publication meets the minimum requirements of
American National Standard for Information Sciences—
Permanence of Paper for Printed Library Materials, ANSI Z39.48-1984.

Subscribers may call customer service at 1-800-558-4343 to make address changes.
Unsolicited manuscripts will not be returned without a self-addressed, stamped envelope.

ISBN 0-8249-1141-5   GST 131903775

Cover Photo: *THE CHRISTMAS TEA SHOPPE.*
Linda Nelson Stocks, artist.

Inside Covers: *SKATING ON CHRISTMAS EVE* (detail).
Linda Nelson Stocks, artist.

S0-CFO-563

Christmas Eve

Laura Hope Wood

The snow began to fall as twilight deepened
    And swirling flakes fell far into the night.
A fairyland soon covered hill and valley
    As drifts piled high in silence deep and white.
There was no sound to break the evening stillness,
    But just the feel of Christmas all around.
Somehow the joy and peace that comes with giving
    Came with each snowflake as it settled down.
A tall tree trimmed with bright and shining tinsel,
    Through frosted windows such a rosy glow
Of presents wrapped in green and crimson tissue
    And firelight dancing on the floor below.
A holly wreath with bright red, frosted berries
    To greet me as I near the waiting door.
I seem to hear the sound of sleigh bells ringing;
    It's Christmas Eve, and I am home once more.

Chickadee

Alice MacKenzie Swaim

A chickadee
on snow-tipped cedar branch
loosened a tiny avalanche
of shimmering, white stars
then flew in feathered buoyancy
to light on grayed fence bars
and sing to me.

Feather-down of Heaven

Anna Belle Jeffries

Feather-down of heaven
That the angels spill,
Blanket tree and hollow,
Cushion dale and hill,

Amplify the clear shine
Of that burning star,
Soften glaring brightness,
Spread its beauty far,

Hush the hurried footsteps
Of this busy earth,
Muffle all its whisp'ring,
Din, and rowdy mirth,

Swirl the stall in silver
Shed from angels' wings,
Keep the world from waking
The newborn King of kings.

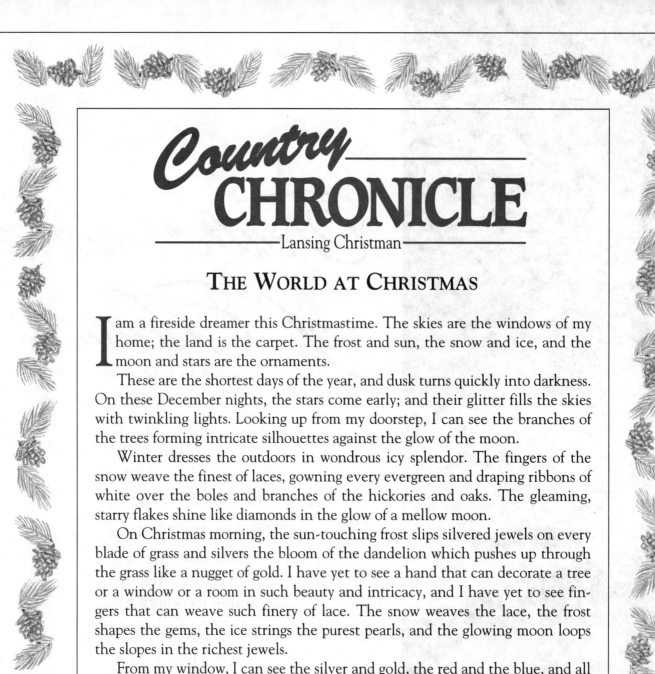

Country CHRONICLE

Lansing Christman

THE WORLD AT CHRISTMAS

I am a fireside dreamer this Christmastime. The skies are the windows of my home; the land is the carpet. The frost and sun, the snow and ice, and the moon and stars are the ornaments.

These are the shortest days of the year, and dusk turns quickly into darkness. On these December nights, the stars come early; and their glitter fills the skies with twinkling lights. Looking up from my doorstep, I can see the branches of the trees forming intricate silhouettes against the glow of the moon.

Winter dresses the outdoors in wondrous icy splendor. The fingers of the snow weave the finest of laces, gowning every evergreen and draping ribbons of white over the boles and branches of the hickories and oaks. The gleaming, starry flakes shine like diamonds in the glow of a mellow moon.

On Christmas morning, the sun-touching frost slips silvered jewels on every blade of grass and silvers the bloom of the dandelion which pushes up through the grass like a nugget of gold. I have yet to see a hand that can decorate a tree or a window or a room in such beauty and intricacy, and I have yet to see fingers that can weave such finery of lace. The snow weaves the lace, the frost shapes the gems, the ice strings the purest pearls, and the glowing moon loops the slopes in the richest jewels.

From my window, I can see the silver and gold, the red and the blue, and all the dazzling and sparkling colors on a tree glowing in all its beauty for the holiday. Outside my door lie the bells, the tinsels, the gems.

Yes, I am a fireside dreamer this holy night. I look up to the skies and the twinkling stars; they are the lamps in the windows of my world, a world designed by God.

The author of two published books, Lansing Christman has been contributing to Ideals *for more than twenty years. Mr. Christman has also been published in several American, foreign, and braille anthologies. He lives in rural South Carolina.*

TRAVELER'S
Diary

Mildred Smithson

WINTER WONDERLAND
Glacier National Park, Montana

Winter seems the perfect season to visit Montana's Glacier National Park, for it is a world created and continually shaped by ice. The mountains are not tall compared to the other Rocky Mountain peaks we saw to the north at Banff—most here are no more than ten thousand feet—but they are, nonetheless, spectacular. Their sharp, serrated peaks, towering spires, and abrupt cliffs bear witness to the giant glaciers that gave the park its name.

Every corner of Glacier offers new wonders: high mountain lakes tucked away in craters and basins carved by ice shine a crystal blue; the alpine tundra appears barren from a distance, the dwarfed vegetation presenting the careful observer with a forest in miniature; layers of limestone, sandstone, and mudstone paint a rainbow of red, green, gray, and tan across the rocky peaks and cliffsides. And because Glacier sits astride the Continental Divide, with water on the east side flowing into the Missouri and Mississippi Rivers and water on the west making its way to the Pacific Ocean, two distinct climates can be enjoyed in the park. On the west, moisture-laden air from the Pacific creates a wet and mild zone; but that air, stripped of its moisture by the peaks of the Rockies, arrives on the eastern side dry and cold; the climate there is less forgiving.

This morning, before setting out for a final day in the park, I read a quote by the naturalist John Muir. He said to give a month's worth of exploring time to Glacier National Park. "The time will not be taken from the sum of your life," he assured. "Instead of shortening, it will indefinitely lengthen it. . . ." Later, gazing upon the Garden Wall—a sharp, serrated peak carved out of hard rock by the simultaneous work of two glaciers retreating for years down opposite sides of a mountain—I understood what Muir meant. At Glacier, the watches, clocks, and calendars of our world are meaningless; time here moves at its own magnificent pace.

Winter's Artistry

Beverly J. Anderson

In the beauty of the moonlight,
Snowflakes swirled through frosty air
Covering the earth in ermine.
When the dawn broke bright and fair,
We beheld a picture postcard
Just as far as eye could see;
For our country town was gift-wrapped
By Queen Winter's artistry.

Such a magic transformation
Had transpired overnight
As the tumbling, pristine snowflakes
Wove a coverlet of white.
All the trees were decked in splendor,
And the hills and vales below
Glistened as the golden sunbeams
Shone like diamonds in the snow.

Frozen icicles trimmed branches
In a fairyland of dreams.
Shrubs wore lacy shawls of silver;
Crystal were the brooks and streams.
Mounds of white crowned every rooftop;
Fence posts all donned caps of snow—
Winter's gift of sparkling whiteness,
Tied with Jack Frost's lace and bow.

CHRISTMAS MORNING
Stark, New Hampshire
Gene Ahrens Photography

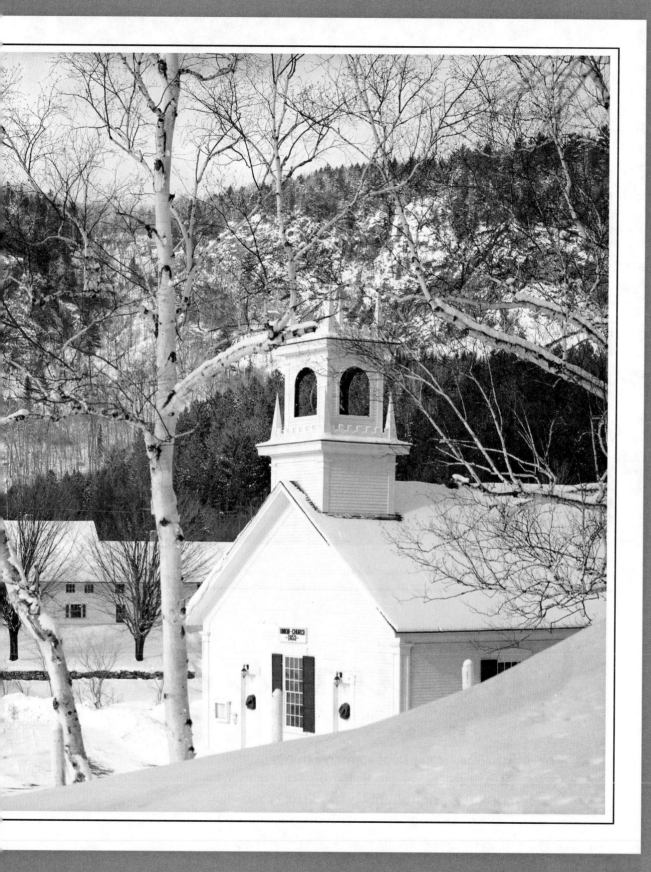

GRAY KITTEN ON CHRISTMAS EVE. Dick Dietrich Photography.

Christmas Is

Virginia Borman Grimmer

Christmas is made of so many things:
Evergreen trees with baubles on strings,
Twinkling bright lights behind frosty panes,
New rocking horses with brown, painted manes,
Peppermint canes and bonbons galore,
Shining red toys just fresh from a store,

RIDING TIGER. Dick Dietrich Photography.

Sunday-school pageants and children aglow,
    Sparkles of ice on crystal white snow.
Fresh cakes a-baking with spices and mace,
    Pretty, dressed dolls in bonnets and lace,
Ribbon-tied gifts all tempting and bright,
    A star-studded sky on Christmas Eve night,
Stockings hung high, awaiting their fill,
    A feeling of warmth, of peace and good will.
Yes, Christmas is made of so many things,
    But mostly of love and the joy that it brings.

Collector's Corner

Jigsaw Puzzles

by Connie L. Flood

Recently, Mary Louise, a young cousin of mine, gave me a gift. She said it was my Christmas present, even though it was more than a month early. Inside an old, battered shoebox lovingly wrapped in the Sunday comics, I found her favorite jigsaw puzzle, one that we had assembled together many times on rainy afternoons at my house. Touched by her gift, I was reminded of many Christmases of my own childhood when my older cousins and I spent hours sifting through piles of cardboard pieces of our Christmas-present puzzles, searching for matching shades of puppy-dog brown or mountain purple. My uncle always gave each of us a puzzle for Christmas, and we spent most of our Florida holidays out on my grandmother's old, roomy, screened-in porch assembling one jigsaw puzzle after another until the porch was carpeted with a mosaic of furry animals and nature scenes. When we finished, we always voted on our favorites before we took the puzzles apart and returned the myriad pieces to their respective boxes.

Now that all of my generation of cousins is grown, we cannot always get together at Christmastime to continue our puzzle-building tradition; but my fond memories of those times gave me a long-lasting affection toward jigsaw puzzles. My basement shelves are full

MYSTIC JIG DETECTIVE NOVEL AND JIG PUZZLE SOLUTION. NO. 1, CROSS EXAMINATION, 1933.
From the collection of Anne Williams. H. L. Rinker, photography.
Courtesy of the Museum of Our National Heritage.

of stacked puzzle boxes; and instead of regular prints or paintings, my walls are decorated with my favorite puzzles, matted and framed for permanent display. Several years ago, I started looking for older puzzles at yard sales and auctions. These puzzles from past days add the most interesting designs and historical appeal to my varied collection.

My prized addition was a puzzle I found in a stack of old games being sold at a yard sale. The puzzle depicts a scene from the nursery rhyme "Little Bo Peep" and dates from the Depression era. Though it is not the prettiest puzzle I have in my collection, "Little Bo Peep" is one of the best loved; and although faded and tattered, it is not missing a single piece. I often think about the child who first owned this puzzle and wonder how many afternoons he or she spent searching for the perfect matching piece of woolly white to complete Bo Peep's sheep.

Perhaps what I love most about collecting jigsaw puzzles is the opportunity to share them with my neighbors and relatives, young and old. Just as in the days of my childhood at my grandmother's house, there is always a puzzle in the works on my front porch; and I love to take the new generation of cousins down to my basement to let them choose their favorites from the boxes stacked on the shelves. As for Mary Louise's puzzle, I keep it close at hand in its shoebox right next to the basement stairs, where it is easy to find when she visits on rainy afternoons.

THE MISSING PIECE

If you would like to start a collection of jigsaw puzzles,
here are some "missing pieces" to help you get started:

PUZZLE FACTS

- Jigsaw puzzles range in size from easy children's puzzles to huge 2,500-piece puzzles.
- Puzzles are made of a variety of materials, but the most popular are wood and cardboard.
- Puzzles can cost anywhere from ten cents for certain Depression-era puzzles to $9,000 for custom-made, specialty puzzles.
- A puzzle's value is greatly diminished if any of its pieces are missing.
- The original box can add value to a puzzle, especially if the box is in pristine condition.

HISTORY

- Jigsaw puzzles were invented in England in the 1760s by a mapmaker named John Spilsbury, who glued engravings of maps to wood backings and sold them as educational tools.
- In the Victorian era, puzzles featuring nursery rhymes and other lighthearted themes gained popularity.
- Puzzles were enjoyed mainly by the wealthy until the invention of the die press, which made puzzles cheaper by allowing them to be mass-produced instead of cut individually by hand.

CLOWN. Wooden puzzle, circa 1908. From the collection of Anne Williams. H. L. Rinker, photography. Courtesy of the Museum of Our National Heritage.

- Puzzles became very popular in America during the Depression because they provided inexpensive entertainment for financially struggling families.

INTERESTING COLLECTIBLES

- Depression-era puzzles, often featuring popular radio or movie characters of the day
- Puzzles with illustrations by famous artists such as Thomas Nast or Dr. Seuss
- Puzzles picturing fine art prints or three-dimensional images
- Mahogany puzzles in the form of personalized silhouettes
- Japanese puzzles, only three inches square, that come with tweezers to assemble their tiny pieces
- Specialty puzzles that can fit together dozens of different ways
- Puzzles that are packaged with a mystery story and provide clues or solutions to the mysteries

CHRISTMAS NIGHT

Oliver Goldsmith

I open the door with stealth and care,
   Scarcely knowing what I'll find there
To lift my heart as I trace with joy
   The treasured trail of my little boy.

His tiny dog stands guard at the stair,
   Minus its tail and part of its hair;
And off in the dim-lit corner hall
   Has rolled his big red rubber ball;
And Venetian blinds hang just the way
   He left them at the close of day.

Houses of blocks are what I meet,
    Constructed right on my favorite seat;
And here's his bib with a generous trace
    Of a lovable smear from his happy face.
Things are upset wherever he's been,
    And tomorrow he'll start all over again.

But now, upstairs, his toddling charms
    Are safely tucked in the sandman's arms.
God, let him continue to spread disarray;
    And thanks for touching our home this way.

Readers' Reflections

THE MEANING OF CHRISTMAS

From out of my memories
In thought I can see
The family at Christmas
And our freshly cut tree.

We had not much money
For bright finery;
But that didn't matter
To us children, you see.

We strung up some popcorn
And tied gingham bows.
Beauty is in the eye;
So the old saying goes.

As for us children,
We were proud of our tree;
For it held the meaning
Of what Christmas should be—

Giving and sharing
Your heart and your love.
For that was the first gift
Sent from heaven above.

So let's not forget
What Christmas does mean;
It's not about presents,
But to honor a King.

Betty Harper Rohr
Buckhannon, West Virgi

LEGACY

The smell of pine invades the house;
There are boxes on the floor.
As Dad untangles all the lights,
We garland every door.
The day I love has come at last,
This time of memory
As we again relate the past
While putting up the tree.
Yes, with each bell, each ball, each star,
We stop and reminisce
Of Christmas trees we've had before
And times and friends we miss.
The paper chain from grammar school,
The wishbone painted red,

The eggshells dipped in glitter,
The tiny wooden sled—
Each bring to mind a story
As we place them one by one.
The shadows lengthen into night
Long before we're done.
Someday the children will be gone,
Each with their own family;
They'll add to the holiday stories
As they put up their tree.
And when the year comes to an end,
They'll pack their treasures away;
And another generation
Will remember the past of today.

Benna Boutty
Geneva, Florida

CHRISTMAS IN MY MEMORY

Cinnamon and evergreen,
A porcelain nativity scene,
Sparkling lights smile on the tree—
I see Christmas in my memory.

I sense an ache, a desperate urge
For Christmas past to gently purge
My longing for the bygone day,
To be again the child at play.

Then Grandma would be here once more
To take us to the ten-cent store,
And Santa's bells on Christmas Eve
Would jingle as his sleigh took leave.

Those Christmases, forever white,
Held magic rife on Christmas night!
Oh, to be a child once more—
I watch now from a distant shore.

Gingerbread and scented pine,
Christmas lights still brightly shine;
My children's eyes glow with delight,
For Christmas is a joyous sight!

I travel from across the shore
To feel my Christmases once more;
Through their resplendent eyes I see
The Christmas in my memory.

Diana Loski
Boise, Idaho

RELUCTANT SHEPHERD

I won't be in the pageant.
I won't even go.
I should be Joseph or a king
Or in the angel chorus sing.
But was I chosen? No!
I'd have to dress in Dad's old robe
And hold that crooked stick.
The dusty sheep of batting
Would probably make me sick.

Still . . .
Christmas needs a shepherd
Mom says, a kid like me
With cowlick and freckles
And bandage on his knee.
She said the Bible shepherds
Were sharp-eyed,
But not real clean,
Though fast, to run to Bethlehem;
They got there first, I mean.

So . . .
I guess I'll play a shepherd
For the third year in a row.
I like that Baby's story,
And the cast gets lunch,
You know.

Nancy Shearin Willis
Louisville, Kentucky

Fifth Street Hill

Jon N. McCready

If you ever went sledding
    On Fifth Street Hill,
You'll remember the challenge,
    Remember the thrill.
The moment the runners
    Were laid on the track,
It was "Look out below!";
    There was no turning back.

From Avenue B
    Down to Avenue A,
Fifth Street would be closed
    For the children to play.
The bobsleds, the flyers,
    Occasional skis
Would soon be appearing
    When Fifth Street would freeze.

The nights, cold and crisp
    With the temperature drop,
And new fallen snow
    Firmly packed at the top
Heightened anticipation
    While waiting in line
For the ride to the bottom
    That stiffened your spine.

The pitch of the hill
    Sent you speeding below
With watering eyes
    From the wind and the snow.
Numb hands gripped the steerage
    To keep her on course
As you fought to control
    Gravitational force.

Much faster and faster,
    You felt you could fly.
Those climbing the hill
    Were a blur passing by.
It took concentration
    To focus your mind,
With a sled out in front
    And another behind.

At last reaching bottom,
    But still running strong,
You just let her coast
    For another block long.
When finally stopped
    And back on your feet,
You began your return
    Up the hill of Fifth Street.

The trudge to the top
    Had its special reward,
There to gather with friends
    Round the fire that roared
From an old metal barrel
    Where people could bend
Just to work out the kinks
    While they warmed either end.

The streetlight that hung
    On the corner would glow
Like a Charles Dickens scene
    With the fresh falling snow.
You drank cups of chocolate
    To help ease the chill
While you watched and you planned
    Your last run down the hill.

It's now just a memory;
    The city won't close
The street any longer
    Whenever it snows.
Concern for your safety
    Has ended the thrill
Of gathering and sledding
    Upon Fifth Street Hill.

22

Remember When

THE CHRISTMAS QUILT

Joyce Ayres

Christmas has always held a special magic for me, but one Christmas still stands out in my memory. I had just turned five, and the holiday season was fresh and exciting for me. My sister Nola and I counted the days until Christmas morning.

Our mother was an avid quilter, and during the Christmas season she always had a special quilt to finish for the family. She spent hours and hours piecing and stitching in the room upstairs where she kept her quilting frames. Every spare moment, Mother could be found creating her own artistic masterpiece from the multi-colored scraps of cloth that would become another quilt. Nola and I would watch in anticipation as another new quilt was finished.

One afternoon Nola and I walked to the nearest store, following the railroad tracks all the way since I loved to "walk the rails." We arrived at the store, all red cheeked from our walk, and began to explore the shop for any new items that may have been added since our last visit. In the rear of the store, behind the enclosed, glass display case, sat a row of baby dolls. They were beautiful! I stared in amazement at the delicate faces, some surrounded by black hair, others with blond curls. One in particular immediately caught my eye. It was a newborn doll dressed in pink bunting, her tearful face crying just like a real baby. I wanted her so much, and I imagined myself gently holding her in my old walnut rocking chair.

"Oh, I want that doll!" I exclaimed eagerly.

Nola bent down to examine my choice. "I like this one," she said, pointing to a black-haired doll sitting near mine.

"Maybe Santa Claus will bring it to you," I answered.

Nola shook her head. "No, they are much too expensive," she said. Nola understood better than I did what the grownups meant when they said "Depression."

Even though my sister was older and wiser, I was sure that the doll I wanted would be waiting for me on Christmas morning. Before we left the store, I took one last look at "my doll."

"Santa Claus will bring it to me. I've been good," I assured myself as we walked down the store steps. My sister merely shook her head.

When we got home, I ran to my mother to tell her about the doll that Santa was going to bring me. Nola described her doll too, but I could tell by the way she talked that she didn't expect to get it. At my age, I didn't realize that Mother and Dad were having trouble putting food on the table, let alone worrying about Christmas.

As November turned to December and Christmas crept closer and closer, I was caught up in the excitement of the holidays. Dad brought home a Christmas tree that he had chopped down in the mountains, and we decorated it with the old Christmas decorations.

A few days before Christmas, Mother was finished with her latest quilt. I remember thinking it was peculiar that she folded the quilt carefully and placed it in a paper bag instead of in the cedar chest where her other quilts were kept; but the festivities of the season distracted me, and I forgot to ask her about the paper bag.

Soon it was Christmas Eve, and my sister and I hung our stockings in anticipation. They were old nylon stockings with runs in them, but we didn't care. They would stretch a long way when Santa filled them with apples, oranges, tangerines, nuts, and hard candy. That night we climbed into bed all warm and snug from the heavy pile of quilts Mother had spread over us; and before long, I was sound asleep.

On Christmas morning, I awoke at dawn. Beside me, resting in the crook of my arm, lay my baby doll, as beautiful as I remembered. I looked at my sister, who was still asleep beside me, and saw she held the black-haired doll she had wanted. It was a moment I will never forget.

Years later I learned that Mother had sold her beautiful quilt to earn enough money to make our Christmas unforgettable. Whenever I'm feeling sentimental, I unwrap the doll from long ago and think of a mother's love, devotion, and sacrifice that made that Christmas moment possible.

HASKINS FAMILY QUILT, circa 1870. Courtesy of Shelburne Museum, Shelburne, Vermont. Photograph by Ken Burris.

Christmas Visitor

Edgar Daniel Kramer

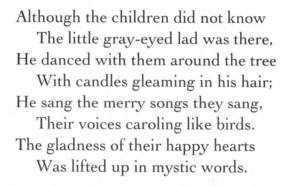

Although the children did not know
   The little gray-eyed lad was there,
He danced with them around the tree
   With candles gleaming in his hair;
He sang the merry songs they sang,
   Their voices caroling like birds.
The gladness of their happy hearts
   Was lifted up in mystic words.

But when the children turned from play
   As weariness led them to bed,
He found me in my easy chair
   And pressed his cheek upon my head;
He snuggled close and, starry-eyed,
   He sighed, "I love our Christmas tree!"
Then fell asleep safe in my arms—
   The little lad I used to be!

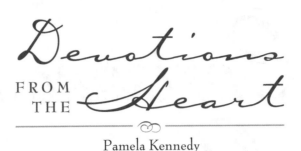

Devotions

FROM
THE
Heart

Pamela Kennedy

Every good gift and every perfect gift is from above, and cometh down from the Father of lights, with whom is no variableness, neither shadow of turning.

–James 1:17

THE PERFECT GIFT

Christmas afternoon is always a time of rest and relaxation at our house. The packages have been opened, our traditional breakfast of *Julekake* is over, and everyone seems busy enjoying his or her Christmas gifts. When our children were younger, the afternoon was usually spent on the living room floor putting together one of those "some assembly required" toys. One year it was a command center for the latest action figures. Another year, the "dream house" for my daughter's fashion doll was under construction most of the day.

When the children grew older, their likes and dislikes became more complex. I was never sure if a sweater would be the shade of blue that was "in" that year or if the computer accessory was compatible. Many Christmas afternoons I realized with disappointment that I had missed the mark with my gifts for the family. After all, I had searched for just the right thing and anticipated how much it would be enjoyed. It seemed a perfect gift, but it wasn't. As much as I love my children and husband, I don't always know all their preferences or needs.

Sometimes I feel as my children do about the gifts my heavenly Father gives to me. I suspect He doesn't know me very well, or He would have given me something different. Yet the Scriptures tell me His gifts are always perfect and good. How can this be? Although my understanding of my own children is limited, God knows me better than I know myself. In His infinite wisdom, He gives me just the right thing at just the right time.

When I am impatient and need to learn to wait, He offers me challenges I cannot rush. When I need to learn mercy, He brings situations into my life that cause me to see my own need for forgiveness. When pride raises its ugly head, I am offered the opportunity to be humbled. When I'm tempted to go my own way, He grants me an experience I cannot handle without His help. What good and perfect gifts these are—how exquisitely matched to my unique needs.

There are times, however, when I want to send His gifts back for another size or shape or even return them unopened. To accept the gift means I must also accept the responsibility to use it, to grow from it, to even learn to be grateful for it. It is not always easy to receive graciously the gifts God sends.

I wonder if Mary and Joseph may have felt a bit uneasy when they received the ultimate gift of God, His only begotten Son. However marvelous and miraculous, it was certainly a complicated gift. How grateful they must have been for the Magi's lavish gifts of gold and frankincense and myrrh, but did they question God's wisdom when He sent them to Egypt on short notice with a tiny child and no reservations? Through the prism of time, however, we recognize how good and perfect God's gifts were to this little family and to the entire family of humankind. The good and perfect gift of God's Son, given that first Christmas long ago, became a blessing for all peoples. For in His infinite wisdom, our heavenly Father, the ultimate gift-giver, knew the size of our need precisely.

Prayer: Dear Lord, at Christmastime and always, help me to graciously accept the gifts of opportunity and blessing sent from Your hand.

Christmas Shoppers

Aileen Fisher

Oh, the wind is brisk and biting,
And the cold is not inviting;
But there's music, merry music everywhere.
All the streets are full of bustle,
And our feet are full of hustle;
For there's Christmas, merry Christmas in the air.

Oh, the wind is cold and chilly,
And it whistles at us shrilly;
But there's music, merry music everywhere.
Chiming bells are full of ringing,
And our hearts are full of singing;
For there's Christmas, merry Christmas in the air.

HANDMADE HEIRLOOM

VICTORIAN CRAZY PATCHWORK CHRISTMAS STOCKING. Crafted by Mary Skarmeas. Jerry Koser Photography.

VICTORIAN CRAZY PATCHWORK CHRISTMAS STOCKING

Mary Skarmeas

Some of my most vivid childhood memories center around the Christmas season; they are warm and happy memories that return each year as autumn turns to winter and the sky and temperature hint of the first snowfall.

The wonderful days between Thanksgiving and Christmas were full of tradition in my childhood home: picking out a tree, unpacking the ornaments, setting up the nativity scene, and falling asleep watching Papa untangle strings of beautiful lights. My younger sister and I especially anticipated the December day when Mama would pull out a box of the prettiest of last year's cards, wrappings, and rib-

bons. From these recycled holiday odds and ends—with additions from Mama's sewing basket full of rickrack, lace, scraps of fabric, ribbon, and braid—we would make a Christmas collage. With scissors and glue and the unlimited imagination of childhood, we created our own unique Christmas decoration, which Mama always proudly displayed throughout the holiday season. I remembered these cherished Christmas collages when I set about to make a Victorian crazy patchwork Christmas stocking. Crazy patchwork is, after all, a collage of fabric color and texture that, like the most simple of childhood creations, is inspired not by a pattern but by an unfettered imagination.

The Victorians made an elegant art of crazy patchwork, piecing together the most beautiful silk, velvet, lace, satin, and brocade; yet the craft's true beginnings are far more humble. When European settlers first came to America, they brought with them hand-sewn quilts. As these quilts began to wear from daily use, they required patching. Fabric, however, was hard to come by. The first commercial fabric mill in the United States did not begin operation until 1815, and imported fabric was scarce and expensive. Early settlers patched their old quilts with scraps of reusable fabric from discarded clothing. Of necessity, the scraps were of all shapes, sizes, patterns, textures, and colors. The quilts that resulted after years of such patching came to be known as crazy patchwork quilts.

This style born of necessity soon became fashionable in its own right. Quilters discovered that such crazy quilts were a perfect showcase for their stitching skills and an outlet for a little bit of creative spirit. By the Victorian era, the crazy patchwork quilt was produced purely for decorative reasons. Quilters pieced together their quilts from every possible shape cut from the finest fabric available. The pieces were joined and then embellished by the quilters' best fancy stitchwork. In an era given to decoration and ornamentation, crazy patchwork found favor.

In addition to offering quilters an opportunity to showcase their stitches, crazy quilts became true historical documents, chronicling a family's past through bits of fabric. The maker might include heirlooms from her past generations, scraps reminiscent of a special occasion or overseas trip, or even a bit from a favorite party dress. Each scrap would be carefully added to the motley pattern then adorned with names, dates, and phrases, all telling a part of a family's unique story and preserving it for another generation.

Today, we more often find crazy patchwork in small projects—wall hangings, table runners, place mats, and, of course, Christmas stockings. And we can replace much of the fancy stitching of the Victorian era with the many lovely trimming accessories that are available: ribbons, laces, braids, and more. The Victorian crazy patchwork style is perfectly suited to a Christmas stocking. The rich reds and greens, the sparkling golds and silvers, the delicate laces, creamy satins, and lush velvets of the Victorian era are at home in any Christmas decor; and they have an old-fashioned appeal that fits in well during a season of memories and tradition.

Basic sewing skills and perhaps a little experience with quilting—or at least a good book of beginners' instruction in the craft—are all that is necessary to create a one-of-a-kind Victorian crazy patchwork Christmas stocking. The stocking has a patchwork front, a rich velvet backing, and a satin lining, along with a muslin interfacing. Get some help from an instruction book for the proper manner of joining the quilt pieces and for the correct method of stitching together the body of the stocking, but don't be discouraged by a lack of sewing experience; the true art of this stocking is the quilted front, which is created by pure whimsy. Draw a basic stocking outline on paper and then divide it into shapes as you see fit. These shapes become the pattern pieces; use them to cut from as many different colors, styles, and textures of fabric as you like. Deep reds and greens, rich brocades, plush velvets, and silky satins will give your stocking a Victorian flavor. When all the piecing is done, finishing work can be done with your finest embroidery stitches, or, like I have done, with a variety of trimmings that complement the colors and textures of the patchwork.

As I worked on my patchwork stocking, I was transported back through time to Mama's kitchen table. I could hear her quiet voice in the background as she went about her daily chores, and I could see my sister sitting beside me, both of us hard at work on our Christmas collage. So many of my most cherished memories center around family traditions, especially holiday traditions. My mother taught me to create beauty out of a box of odds and ends from a Christmas past. Making this stocking, which in its rich Victorian colors and textures reminds me so much of the things that Mama held dear, was a tribute to her memory. Some day, I hope, this stocking will hang in the home of one of my own children and remind them of cold December days and the warmth of our family Christmases.

Mary Skarmeas lives in Danvers, Massachusetts, and has recently earned her bachelor's degree in English at Suffolk University. Mother of four and grandmother of two, Mary loves all crafts, especially knitting.

Three Gifts

Vic Jameson

God gave a child,
And in a manger lay the priceless gift of all eternity:
A sleeping babe, unheralded by rulers of a restless world except for three
Who saw the everlasting hope of men
In a humble crib, in Bethlehem.

God gave a star
And by its light displayed a path for wandering shepherd folk to see
A Saviour child, unknown to millions heedless of the destiny
Of a soundless infant in repose,
Lying in a stall, in swaddling clothes.

God gave a song;
And angel legions sang the haunting phrases of a melody
That never ends and lifted from a tiny town's obscurity
A boy child born in a mound of hay
To give a waiting world its Christmas Day.

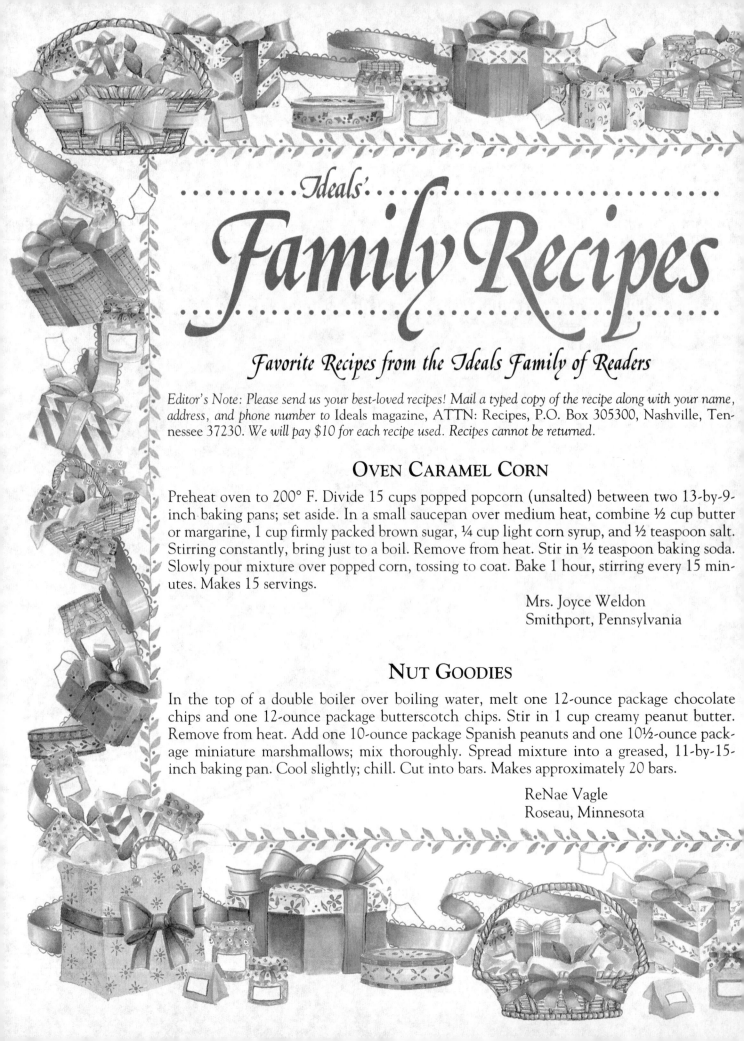

Ideals' Family Recipes

Favorite Recipes from the Ideals Family of Readers

Editor's Note: Please send us your best-loved recipes! Mail a typed copy of the recipe along with your name, address, and phone number to Ideals magazine, ATTN: Recipes, P.O. Box 305300, Nashville, Tennessee 37230. We will pay $10 for each recipe used. Recipes cannot be returned.

OVEN CARAMEL CORN

Preheat oven to 200° F. Divide 15 cups popped popcorn (unsalted) between two 13-by-9-inch baking pans; set aside. In a small saucepan over medium heat, combine ½ cup butter or margarine, 1 cup firmly packed brown sugar, ¼ cup light corn syrup, and ½ teaspoon salt. Stirring constantly, bring just to a boil. Remove from heat. Stir in ½ teaspoon baking soda. Slowly pour mixture over popped corn, tossing to coat. Bake 1 hour, stirring every 15 minutes. Makes 15 servings.

Mrs. Joyce Weldon
Smithport, Pennsylvania

NUT GOODIES

In the top of a double boiler over boiling water, melt one 12-ounce package chocolate chips and one 12-ounce package butterscotch chips. Stir in 1 cup creamy peanut butter. Remove from heat. Add one 10-ounce package Spanish peanuts and one 10½-ounce package miniature marshmallows; mix thoroughly. Spread mixture into a greased, 11-by-15-inch baking pan. Cool slightly; chill. Cut into bars. Makes approximately 20 bars.

ReNae Vagle
Roseau, Minnesota

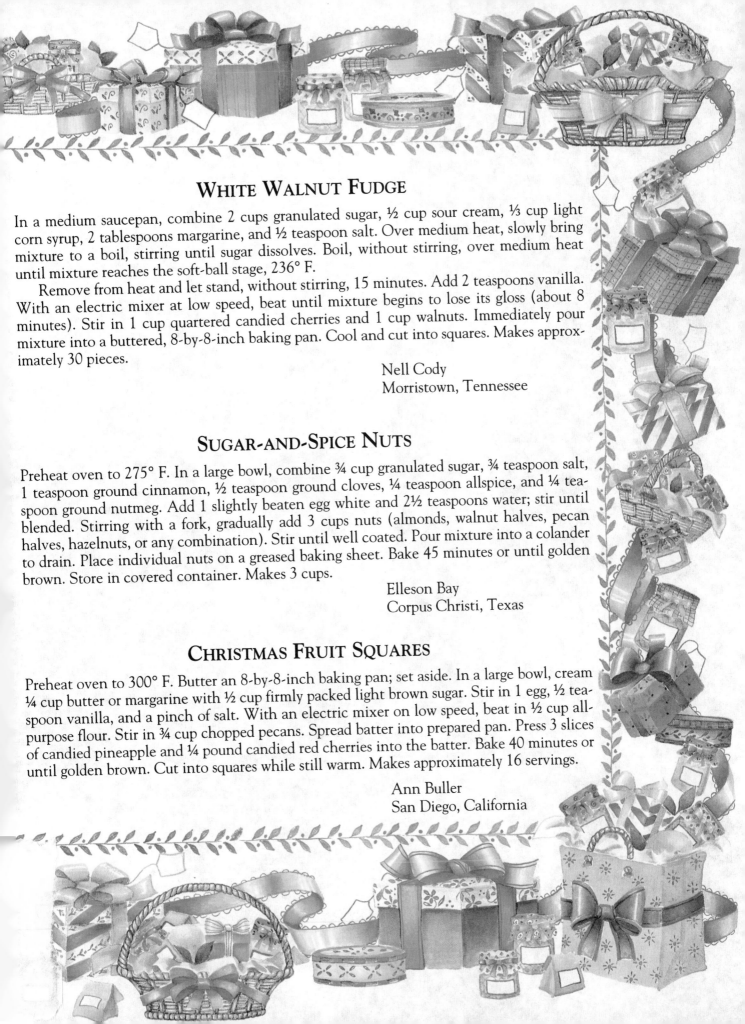

White Walnut Fudge

In a medium saucepan, combine 2 cups granulated sugar, ½ cup sour cream, ⅓ cup light corn syrup, 2 tablespoons margarine, and ½ teaspoon salt. Over medium heat, slowly bring mixture to a boil, stirring until sugar dissolves. Boil, without stirring, over medium heat until mixture reaches the soft-ball stage, 236° F.

Remove from heat and let stand, without stirring, 15 minutes. Add 2 teaspoons vanilla. With an electric mixer at low speed, beat until mixture begins to lose its gloss (about 8 minutes). Stir in 1 cup quartered candied cherries and 1 cup walnuts. Immediately pour mixture into a buttered, 8-by-8-inch baking pan. Cool and cut into squares. Makes approximately 30 pieces.

Nell Cody
Morristown, Tennessee

Sugar-and-Spice Nuts

Preheat oven to 275° F. In a large bowl, combine ¾ cup granulated sugar, ¾ teaspoon salt, 1 teaspoon ground cinnamon, ½ teaspoon ground cloves, ¼ teaspoon allspice, and ¼ teaspoon ground nutmeg. Add 1 slightly beaten egg white and 2½ teaspoons water; stir until blended. Stirring with a fork, gradually add 3 cups nuts (almonds, walnut halves, pecan halves, hazelnuts, or any combination). Stir until well coated. Pour mixture into a colander to drain. Place individual nuts on a greased baking sheet. Bake 45 minutes or until golden brown. Store in covered container. Makes 3 cups.

Elleson Bay
Corpus Christi, Texas

Christmas Fruit Squares

Preheat oven to 300° F. Butter an 8-by-8-inch baking pan; set aside. In a large bowl, cream ¼ cup butter or margarine with ½ cup firmly packed light brown sugar. Stir in 1 egg, ½ teaspoon vanilla, and a pinch of salt. With an electric mixer on low speed, beat in ½ cup all-purpose flour. Stir in ¾ cup chopped pecans. Spread batter into prepared pan. Press 3 slices of candied pineapple and ¼ pound candied red cherries into the batter. Bake 40 minutes or until golden brown. Cut into squares while still warm. Makes approximately 16 servings.

Ann Buller
San Diego, California

Christmas Candle

Kay Hoffman

Light a Christmas candle
   And let it warmly glow
From out a friendly windowpane
   Across new-fallen snow.

Someone lone in passing
   Will catch the strong, bright beam
To cheer the rugged path ahead
   And set the heart to dream.

Let the warm, glad light-shine
   From your own candle's ray
Glow deep within your loving heart
   On each and every day.

Light a Christmas candle
   To glow within your heart
And touch the life of someone dear
   With blessings to impart.

My Favorite Christmas Memory

Personal Stories of Treasured Memories from the Ideals Family of Readers

A Joyous Christmas Carol

On that December morning of 1949, our family and others crowded into the vestibule of the old country church. The men stamped snow off their shoes and greeted their neighbors with comments about the weather. The women nodded and spoke quietly while helping their children struggle out of heavy coats, making sure mittens were tucked securely in pockets. No one spoke of the new family expected that day.

The simple meeting hall echoed with the sounds of shoes on the wooden floor as everyone settled into the timeworn pews. I outmaneuvered my younger brother to sit on the aisle so I could see the strangers in the front pew sitting with Joyce Stevens and her parents.

Excitement and curiosity ran on muted whispers aisle to aisle and row to row in the large square room. On this, the fifth Christmas since the end of World War II, it finally happened. The refugee family had arrived!

I studied the young couple sitting quietly in their drab, worn clothes. The wife's dark hair was nearly hidden by a shapeless felt hat of indistinct gray. Beside her were a little boy and an older couple who I'd been told were her parents.

The family had been driven from their home in the Ukraine to a refugee camp in Germany. There the young man and woman had met, married and had a son. Their resettlement to the United States had been delayed by the wife's refusal to leave her parents behind.

They were here in the middle of Iowa because the Stevenses had offered sponsorship, housing, and work on their farm. For the past few weeks, church members had worked to fix up the old tenant house and scurried around gathering furniture, bedding, and clothing. They raided their freezer lockers and pantries for meat and home-canned fruit and vegetables.

As the worship service began, the minister stood and welcomed the newcomers. They lifted their heads in polite attention, but we knew only the husband spoke a few words of English. They listened to the sermon with disciplined interest, however, and their eyes never wandered.

Finally, we rose for the closing hymn. The young husband dutifully took the open hymnal offered him by Mr. Stevens. Then I saw him turn to his wife and point to something on the page. She brightened and nudged her parents. Alert, they listened to the prelude.

We turned toward the family in surprise as we realized they were singing with us, but in their own language. Smiles broke across the room in waves, and I felt the lift of joy as our voices blended in the last verses of the carol *"Stille Nacht"* ("Silent Night").

Lorene Hoover
Ames, Iowa

The Wonder Box

When I was young, my mother, father, and my five brothers and sisters and I lived in northern Minnesota. Each Christmas, we eagerly looked for the usual big box of Christmas gifts we always received from our grandma, grandpa, and aunt who lived in Milwaukee, Wisconsin. One year the postman left yet another box from Milwaukee on our doorstep a few days before Christmas. We all wondered what treasures the box could possibly be hiding.

When Christmas morning arrived, we were more interested in what was in the mysterious box than in our gifts under the tree. When Dad finally opened it, we were delighted to find it filled with colorful, old-fashioned ribbon candy, delicious red raspberry candies, filled peppermint candies, and all kinds of cookies.

For several more Christmases, the "wonder box" became a much-enjoyed and anticipated Christmas tradition. Each child would take his or her favorite pieces of candy and look for the little trinkets my aunt tucked in for each of us.

Several years ago I received an unexpected package from my older sister. On top was a note asking, "Do you remember the wonder box?" Inside was a Christmas tree ornament shaped like a tiny sled. On it, my sister had printed "Flexible Flyer," the sled that was our pride and joy when we were small. The gift was surrounded by a colorful array of sweets, just like the special gifts that we discovered in my aunt's wonder boxes. My sister's modern wonder box brought back such fond and loving memories of many happy childhood Christmases.

Mrs. Robert Adams
Sheboygan, Wisconsin

The Christmas Visitor

It was about nine o'clock in the morning on Christmas Day 1930, and Mom and Sis were chattering in the kitchen. I, an eight-year-old boy, had finished my first assault on Santa's packages when a sudden knock rattled the screen door on our rear porch.

Our house was the second one from the railroad on the east side of our small rural village, and drifters were sometimes seen lingering nearby as they waited for the next passing train. Soon after I heard the knock on the back door, Sis exclaimed, "Mother, there's a strange man out there, a hobo or a tramp."

"Oh dear, Dad's not here," Mom muttered, as I followed her onto the porch.

"What do you want?" she asked the visitor as she hooked the screen door.

"A cup of coffee, please, ma'am, and maybe something to eat?" He looked her right in the eye while perching one foot on the porch step.

Mom handed the man a steaming cup of coffee and rehooked the screen door. We silently huddled inside the kitchen doorway, waiting for him to finish the cup.

"What are we going to do?" blurted Sis.

"Well, we can't leave him outside; and besides, it's Christmas," Mom said, and she ushered him into the kitchen.

Seated at the table, the man began to tell of his travels from Louisiana into Canada. Sis scurried about, keeping his coffee warm. Mom made him breakfast, now and then sitting to listen to a gripping part of one of his stories.

Raising his eyes at the sound of a distant train whistle, the visitor soon announced that he had to go. As Mom let him out the back door, he paused. "Madam, may the blessings of this Christmas Day be yours," he said gently.

And this time, Mom did not hook the screen door.

Robert L. Swartzel
Kettering, Ohio

Editor's Note: Do you have a special holiday or seasonal memory that you'd like to share with the Ideals family of readers? We'd love to read it! Send your typed memory to:

MY FAVORITE MEMORY
C/O EDITORIAL DEPARTMENT
IDEALS MAGAZINE
535 METROPLEX DRIVE, SUITE 250
NASHVILLE, TENNESSEE 37211

A SLICE OF LIFE

Edgar A. Guest

First Christmas Eve

Only a stable and straw for her bed,
    And no one to notice the star overhead;
And only poor shepherds the Christ Child to see,
    Who had heard that His cradle a manger would be.

How strangely God's purpose is hidden from men!
    They were merely two travel-worn wanderers then.

Just Joseph and Mary in pitiful plight,
    A stall in a stable her chamber that night.

No heralds with trumpets the Prince to receive,
    No welcome by cannon that first Christmas Eve.
Just Joseph and Mary, with straw for her bed;
    A Babe in a manger, a star overhead.

Edgar A. Guest began his illustrious career in 1895 at the age of fourteen when his work first appeared in the Detroit Free Press. His column was syndicated in over three hundred newspapers, and he became known as "The Poet of the People."

Patrick McRae is an artist who lives in the Milwaukee, Wisconsin, area. He has created nostalgic artwork for Ideals for more than a decade, and his favorite models are his wife and three children.

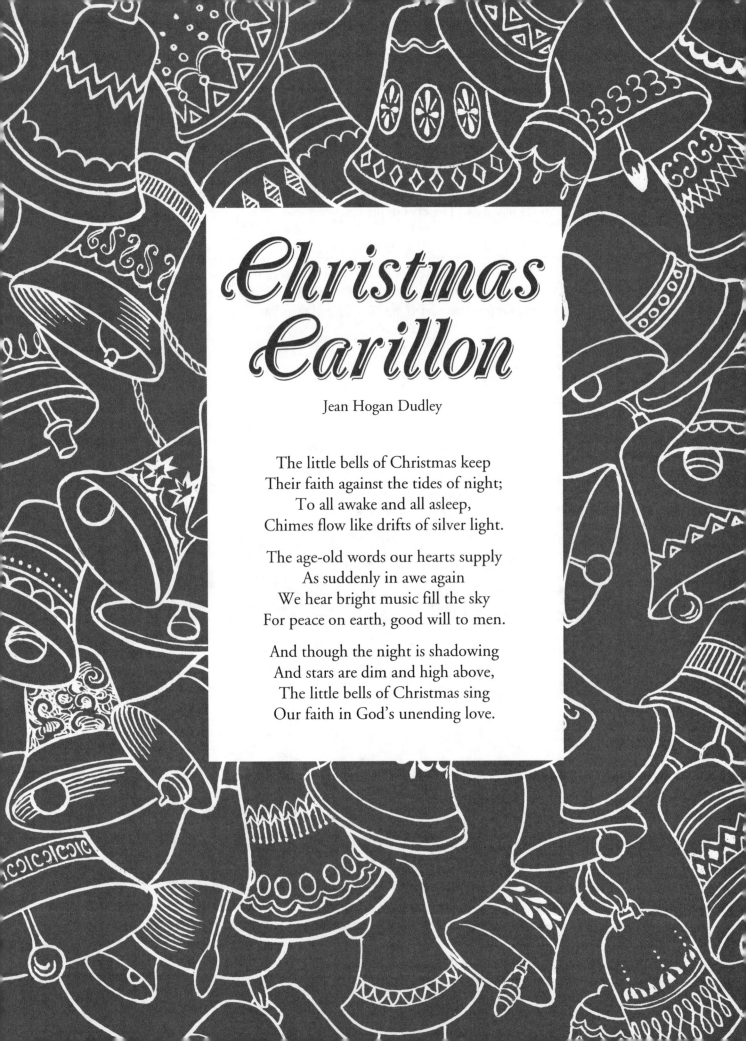

Christmas Carillon

Jean Hogan Dudley

The little bells of Christmas keep
Their faith against the tides of night;
To all awake and all asleep,
Chimes flow like drifts of silver light.

The age-old words our hearts supply
As suddenly in awe again
We hear bright music fill the sky
For peace on earth, good will to men.

And though the night is shadowing
And stars are dim and high above,
The little bells of Christmas sing
Our faith in God's unending love.

Christmas Bells

Beverly J. Anderson

O Christmas bells, glad Christmas bells,
Ring out the news your music tells.
Tell of that bright and shining star
That led the wise men from afar,
Tell of the shepherds on the hill
That holy night so hushed and still.

O Christmas bells, glad Christmas bells,
Ring out the news your music tells.
Peal out your message o'er the earth
That hearts of all may know rebirth.
And as your loud hosannas ring,
May humankind proclaim Christ King!

FOR THE CHILDREN

ARTWORK BY RUSS FLINT

WHEN MARY...

Rachel Field

When Mary rode with Joseph
   And frost was in the air,
And all the roads were crowded,
   And no room anywhere—
Most welcome must the stable roof
   Have loomed that sheltered her,
The scent of hay and straw more sweet
   Than Magi's gift of myrrh.

When Mary heard the singing
   Of far, angelic band,
She trembled at those solemn words
   She could not understand.
The tidings they were telling
   Were thorns upon her breast—
It was the doves' familiar sound
   That set her heart at rest.

When Mary left the stable
   With Joseph at her side,
An angel led the way before
   To guard her newborn pride.
But Mary turned her head away
   From heights of paradise
To bless a manger filled with hay
   And humble, watching eyes.

How Wonderful

John C. Bonser

How wonderful, as waiting ends,
That men and angels meet as friends
To celebrate the Christ Child's birth
As starry peace descends to earth

To bathe with light an ancient town
That will forever be renowned!

How wonderful a manger holds
A King, not clad in silks and golds,
But rather wrapped in swaddling clothes
No court's designer ever chose

And that a stable's rustic walls
Supplant some mansion's stately halls!

How wonderful that wise men three
Should see at once His deity
While humble shepherds hear on high
Joyful hosannas pierce the sky!

More wonderful, in faith's sunrise—
God's love revealed in Mary's eyes!

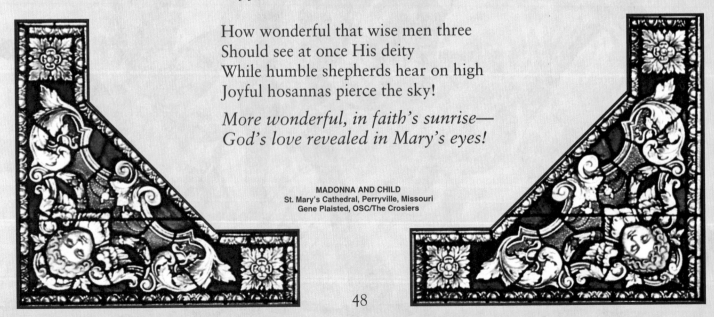

MADONNA AND CHILD
St. Mary's Cathedral, Perryville, Missouri
Gene Plaisted, OSC/The Crosiers

Christmas Eve

Anna Belle Jeffries

Snowflakes fall so gently
On the world tonight,
Touching all with magic,
Robing all in white.
Stars shine in the heavens
Through the lace of snow,
Sending down their blessings
On the earth below.
In the crystal clearness
Of the winter air,
Angel voices echo
In the stillness there.
Down through all the ages,
From the realms on high,
Heaven's music mingles
With my heart's own sigh!
Pure, white silence blankets
Every hill and dale,
So the world can listen
To the angels' tale.
"Holy, Holy, Holy"
Is the song they sing
As again they laud
The newborn King of kings!
Vast as all the cosmos,
Close as my own soul,
God's love, born at Christmas,
Comes to make me whole.
Snowflakes gather softly
On each bush and tree,
Like God's gentle blessings
Fall and cover me!

The ANNUNCIATION

And in the sixth month the angel Gabriel was sent from God unto a city of Galilee, named Nazareth, To a virgin espoused to a man whose name was Joseph, of the house of David; and the virgin's name was Mary.

And the angel came in unto her, and said, Hail, thou that art highly favoured, the Lord is with thee: blessed art thou among women. And when she saw him, she was troubled at his saying, and cast in her mind what manner of salutation this should be.

And the angel said unto her, Fear not, Mary: for thou hast found favour with God. And, behold, thou shalt conceive in thy womb, and bring forth a son, and shalt call his name JESUS. He shall be great, and shall be called the Son of the Highest: and the Lord God shall give unto him the throne of his father David: And he shall reign over the house of Jacob for ever; and of his kingdom there shall be no end.

Luke 1:26-33

THE ANNUNCIATION
Mosaic by Pietro Cavallini, 1250-1330
Santa Maria Church in Trastevere, Rome, Italy
Nimatallah/Art Resource, New York

Mother and Child

And it came to pass in those days, that there went out a decree from Caesar Augustus, that all the world should be taxed. (And this taxing was first made when Cyrenius was governor of Syria.) And all went to be taxed, every one into his own city.

And Joseph also went up from Galilee, out of the city of Nazareth, into Judaea, unto the city of David, which is called Bethlehem; (because he was of the house and lineage of David:) To be taxed with Mary his espoused wife, being great with child.

And so it was, that, while they were there, the days were accomplished that she should be delivered. And she brought forth her firstborn son, and wrapped him in swaddling clothes, and laid him in a manger; because there was no room for them in the inn.

Luke 2:1-7

ADORATION OF THE MAGI (DETAIL)
Mosaic by Pietro Cavallini, 1250-1330
Santa Maria Church in Trastevere, Rome, Italy
Scala/Art Resource, New York

The Nativity

And there were in the same country shepherds abiding in the field, keeping watch over their flock by night. And, lo, the angel of the Lord came upon them, and the glory of the Lord shone round about them: and they were sore afraid.

And the angel said unto them, Fear not: for, behold, I bring you good tidings of great joy, which shall be to all people. For unto you is born this day in the city of David a Saviour, which is Christ the Lord. And this shall be a sign unto you; Ye shall find the babe wrapped in swaddling clothes, lying in a manger. And suddenly there was with the angel a multitude of the heavenly host praising God, and saying, Glory to God in the highest, and on earth peace, good will toward men.

And it came to pass, as the angels were gone away from them into heaven, the shepherds said one to another, Let us now go even unto Bethlehem, and see this thing which is come to pass, which the Lord hath made known unto us. And they came with haste, and found Mary, and Joseph, and the babe lying in a manger. And when they had seen it, they made known abroad the saying which was told them concerning this child. And all they that heard it wondered at those things which were told them by the shepherds. But Mary kept all these things, and pondered them in her heart. And the shepherds returned, glorifying and praising God for all the things that they had heard and seen, as it was told unto them.

Luke 2:8-20

THE NATIVITY
Mosaic by Pietro Cavallini, 1250-1330
Santa Maria Church in Trastevere, Rome, Italy
Scala/Art Resource, New York

The Three Magi

Saying, Where is he that is born King of the Jews? for we have seen his star in the east, and are come to worship him. When Herod the king had heard these things, he was troubled, and all Jerusalem with him. And when he had gathered all the chief priests and scribes of the people together, he demanded of them where Christ should be born.

And they said unto him, In Bethlehem of Judaea: for thus it is written by the prophet, And thou Bethlehem, in the land of Juda, art not the least among the princes of Juda: for out of thee shall come a Governor, that shall rule my people Israel. Then Herod, when he had privily called the wise men, enquired of them diligently what time the star appeared. And he sent them to Bethlehem, and said, Go and search diligently for the young child; and when ye have found him, bring me word again, that I may come and worship him also. When they had heard the king, they departed; and, lo, the star, which they saw in the east, went before them, till it came and stood over where the young child was. When they saw the star, they rejoiced with exceeding great joy.

And when they were come into the house, they saw the young child with Mary his mother, and fell down, and worshipped him: and when they had opened their treasures, they presented unto him gifts; gold, and frankincense, and myrrh. And being warned of God in a dream that they should not return to Herod, they departed into their own country another way.

And when they were departed, behold, the angel of the Lord appeareth to Joseph in a dream, saying, Arise, and take the young child and his mother, and flee into Egypt, and be thou there until I bring thee word: for Herod will seek the young child to destroy him. When he arose, he took the young child and his mother by night, and departed into Egypt:

And was there until the death of Herod: that it might be fulfilled which was spoken of the Lord by the prophet, saying, Out of Egypt have I called my son.

Matthew 2:2-15

The PRESENTATION

AND when eight days were accomplished for the circumcising of the child, his name was called JESUS, which was so named of the angel before he was conceived in the womb. And when the days of her purification according to the law of Moses were accomplished, they brought him to Jerusalem, to present him to the Lord; (As it is written in the law of the Lord, Every male that openeth the womb shall be called holy to the Lord;) And to offer a sacrifice according to that which is said in the law of the Lord, A pair of turtledoves, or two young pigeons.

And, behold, there was a man in Jerusalem, whose name was Simeon; and the same man was just and devout, waiting for the consolation of Israel: and the Holy Ghost was upon him. And it was revealed unto him by the Holy Ghost, that he should not see death, before he had seen the Lord's Christ. And he came by the Spirit into the temple: and when the parents brought in the child Jesus, to do for him after the custom of the law, Then took he him up in his arms, and blessed God, and said, Lord, now lettest thou thy servant depart in peace, according to thy word: For mine eyes have seen thy salvation, Which thou hast prepared before the face of all people; A light to lighten the Gentiles, and the glory of thy people Israel.

And Joseph and his mother marvelled at those things which were spoken of him.

Luke 2:21-33

THE PRESENTATION (DETAIL)
Mosaic by Pietro Cavallini, 1250-1330
Santa Maria Church in Trastevere, Rome, Italy
Scala/Art Resource, New York

Star & Song

Jessie Wilmore Murton

While starlight frosted all the plain,
The quiet hills of Bethlehem
Held close the little sleeping town
That nestled to the heart of them.

And night and silence softly flung
 Their spell of peace and stillness down
About the shepherds and their flocks,
 About the cattle and the town.

No bell pealed out from frescoed spire;
 No carol echoed in the street;
No candlelight at casement glowed,
 The tiny Son of God to greet.

Only the watching shepherds heard
 The song the angels came to sing.
Only three wise men marked the star
 That told the birth night of a King!

LEGENDARY AMERICANS

CONNIE L. FLOOD

MARIA MITCHELL

Throughout her life, Maria Mitchell looked to the stars, studying them and recording her observations in her study of astronomy. But she reached for the stars in another way as well, by becoming the first woman astronomer and inspiring a future generation of young scientists.

Born in 1818 on Nantucket, off the coast of Massachusetts, Maria (pronounced Ma-RYE-ah) Mitchell was the third of William and Lydia Mitchell's ten children. Her family was deeply immersed in the unique culture of Nantucket, with its strong Quaker influence that emphasized hard work, independence, and equality between men and women. The islanders were also closely connected with the sea. In the early nineteenth century, Nantucket was one of the world's most important whaling ports, and a knowledge of the stars was crucial to the town's seafarers who navigated their ships to distant shores.

This acute interest in the stars was evident at the Mitchell household, where Maria's father nightly spent hours on the roof, studying the sky through a small telescope and rating chronometers for the Nantucket whaling fleet by using stellar observations. At a very young age, Maria would join him on the roof, bundled up against the winter cold, and watch the stars with him for hours. When she was only twelve, Maria used a chronometer to count the seconds while her father observed an annular eclipse. Together, they used this and other observations to calculate Nantucket's exact longitude and latitude.

Maria later contributed her interest in astronomy to her father's example. William Mitchell, a schoolmaster, believed in education through observation, a fundamental tenet at his school, which Maria attended as a child. Both at home and in class, Maria was taught the value of observing her world. Always hungering for knowledge, she pored over her studies and overcame her early struggles with mathematics, which later became such an important part of her work. She once said, "I was born of only ordinary capacity, but of extraordinary persistency."

After finishing her schooling, Maria remained on Nantucket with her parents. She soon obtained a job at the Nantucket Atheneum, the recently established library, as the librarian, a post she held for two decades. The job offered Maria endless opportunities to study astronomy and philosophy and even teach herself German. At night, she continued to pursue her favorite pastime—studying the stars.

Maria spent many evenings in her father's conservatory where, side by side, they recorded their observations of the stars and moon. Her father had received a new two-inch Dollond telescope for his work for the United States Coast Survey. One clear October night in 1847, Maria pointed the telescope toward Polaris and discovered a dim, fuzzy patch that did not appear on any of her astronomical charts. After several days of careful observation to absolutely confirm her find and calculate the patch's orbit (a painstaking task in the days before computers), she reported her discovery to the observatory at Harvard University, where scientists confirmed that Maria had discovered a previously unknown comet.

The small fuzzy patch Maria discovered in the sky changed her life forever. The comet was named "Miss Mitchell's Comet" (Comet 1847 VI) in her honor; and the discovery merited her a gold medal from the King of Denmark, who had offered the prize to the first person to discover a telescopic comet (one that could only be seen through a telescope). Maria's discovery earned her national and international recognition as an astronomer. A scientific survey on astronomy included a chapter on Mitchell's findings, and she became the first woman elected both to the American Academy of Arts and Sciences in Boston and the American Association for the Advancement of Science. She was later appointed to the original mathematical computation staff for the newly instituted *American Ephemeris and Nautical Almanac*. Beginning in 1857, Maria spent two years traveling, mostly in Europe, where she reported on her work and met with many noted scientists, who were eager to meet the famous woman astronomer from America.

In 1861, soon after Maria returned to Massachusetts, she received a letter from Matthew Vassar asking if she would consider teaching astronomy at a new women's college he was establishing. Although she had been awarded several honorary college degrees, Maria had no college education; yet because of her tremendous accomplishments in her field, Mr. Vassar was confident in her abilities. In fact, he was so eager to have a woman of Maria's reputation as a part of his first faculty that he offered to build a new observatory for Maria's work. Complete with a new twelve-inch refracting telescope (which Maria believed to be the third best in America), the facility would rival those of Harvard and Yale. Although much of the general public and many of the school's trustees vehemently opposed hiring a woman, Maria faced their criticism to become the first female professor of astronomy; she could not turn down an opportunity to educate young women and encourage their interest in science.

Although Maria Mitchell's research greatly influenced the field of astronomy, many may argue that her greatest work was accomplished while teaching at Vassar. She insisted on the highest standards from her students by requiring rigorous mathematics training and expecting her classes to be highly scientific. Following her father's well-taught principles, she expected her students to learn by observation, not rote. Many of her students adopted her dedication and enthusiasm; night after night, they would work at her side in the conservatory, much like she had with her father years before. Maria left a powerful influence on her students; several went on to study astronomy or other sciences professionally, and twenty-five appear in *Who's Who in America*, a testament to Maria's dedication to promoting women's work in the scientific field.

While at Vassar and throughout the rest of her life, Maria continued her own research. Entries from her detailed journals describe the pleasures and frustrations of observing the stars, of which she once wrote, "No flower garden presents such a variety and such delicacy of shades." She was a pioneer in daily photographing sunspots; and she made significant observations about planetary surfaces and solar eclipses, often reporting her findings in the *American Journal of Science and Arts*.

Maria Mitchell's love for astronomy was equaled by her desire to inspire others' interest in the stars. Her dedication is evidenced today by a thriving program of professional research at the Maria Mitchell Observatory in her beloved Nantucket. The observatory is a rich repository for photographs of variable stars and boasts advanced equipment and research abilities. Perhaps most importantly, the facility offers the public an opportunity to educate themselves and discover the science that so consumed Maria's life.

Maria Mitchell was blessed with an insatiable hunger for understanding her universe. She once wrote, "The world of learning is so broad, and the human soul is so limited in power! We reach forth and strain every nerve, but we seize only a bit of the curtain that hides the infinite from us." Perhaps it was this hunger that gave her the motivation to overcome nineteenth-century stereotypes about women and become one of the leading scientists of her generation. Maria Mitchell died in 1889, yet the effects of her accomplishments are still seen today. Her work not only gave scientists a better understanding of the heavens but also cleared the way for future women scientists to reach for the stars.

Wise Men Still Seek

Kay Hoffman

From out the east the wise men came
    In hurried westward flight;
Across the desert sands they rode,
    Led by the star's pure light.

They carried with them precious gifts
    Fit for a newborn King;
The star proclaimed His royal birth,
    A truly wondrous thing.

They sought Him in a palace grand;
    The star stood still instead
Above a lowly bed of straw
    Within a cattle shed.

But oh, they knew He was their King
    In awesome wonder there;
They laid their treasures at His feet
    And humbly knelt in prayer.

On this night of our Saviour's birth,
    Unknown the path ahead,
Wise men with their bright, guiding star
    Still seek the manger bed.

BITS & PIECES

Christmas began in the heart of God.
It is complete only when it reaches
the heart of man.
—*Author Unknown*

God grant you the light in Christmas, which is faith;
the warmth of Christmas, which is love;
the radiance of Christmas, which is purity;
the righteousness of Christmas, which is justice;
the belief in Christmas, which is truth;
the all of Christmas, which is Christ.
—*Wilda English*

Christmas is the day that holds all time together.
—*Alexander Smith*

Great is the spirit of Christmas that brings
to every heart peace, good will toward all mankind.
—*Horace Wilson*

Holy night, peaceful night,
Wondrous star, lend thy light!
With the angels let us sing
Alleluia to our King;
Jesus the Saviour is here.
—*Joseph Mohr*

Sweet child Jesus, hushaby, hushaby,
On a soft fur you shall lie.
In the cradle gently swinging,
Angel voices gaily singing.
Close your eyes, O Jesus mild,
Mary's son—the sweetest child.
—*18th Century Czechoslovakian Song*

For unto us a child is born, unto us a son is given:
and the government shall be upon his shoulder:
and his name shall be called Wonderful, Counsellor,
The mighty God, The everlasting Father,
The Prince of Peace.
—*Isaiah 9:6*

69

From My
Garden Journal
by Deana Deck

BAYBERRY

The clean, spicy scent of bayberry candles has been part of the Christmas holidays for so long that it may come as a surprise to learn that these aromatic candles are one of the few purely American contributions to an otherwise European tradition. From Germany we inherited the Christmas tree, Scandinavia contributed Saint Nick, England chimed in with yule logs and carol singing, but bayberry candles came to the celebration courtesy of the Native Americans of the Northeast.

When the Pilgrims arrived in the New World, they were dependent for light on greasy, smelly, tallow candles rendered from animal fat. In addition to other survival lore gleaned from Native Americans, the colonists were introduced to the native bayberry bush and taught to capture its clean-burning, fragrant wax for use as a much more pleasant source of light.

Today, although the wild, native bayberry can still be found along coastal dunes from Newfoundland to Maryland, the bush has been tamed and is an important part of the domestic landscape. In the wild, the bush can reach heights of eight to nine feet with an equal spread; but in the backyard garden, the more domesticated cultivars usually do not exceed three to five feet in height and width.

The bayberry takes well to pruning and is easily kept to a desired size for landscape use. Some species are even used as hedges, and all are popular for their ability to grow on dry, sterile soils and in areas where sand and salt keep other plants from thriving. Bayberries require full sun and well draining, acid soil. If your soil is alkaline, you'll need to amend it with acidic compost and perhaps even sulfur. A soil test will determine what to add, and your county agent can suggest the proper amounts.

Mulches of pine needles and peat moss will help hold the soil acidity at a constant level, as will the use of fertilizers formulated for acidic plants. Be sparing with your fertilizer, however, since this plant does not require much. Being a coastal native, bayberry is accustomed to sandy, quickly draining soil. If yours is slow-draining clay, condition it by adding sand and peat moss.

The shrub is easy to propagate from underground stolons (stems) that can be cut from the mother plant. It can also be started from rooted offshoots or softwood cuttings in late spring or early summer. A difficult species to transplant from the wild, the bayberry's survival rate is best when purchased container-grown or balled and burlapped from a reputable nursery.

In all species of *Myrica*, there are separate male and female plants. Their appearance is identical, and the only way you can tell the female plants from the male plants is that only the females produce berries. For this reason, it's best to purchase the plants in fall when you can readily identify the females by their berries. For adequate pollination, plant one male for every six to ten females.

Several varieties of *Myrica* do well outside of the New England and mid-Atlantic states. One is the California bayberry (M. *californica*), hardy to areas where temperatures do not drop below 0° F. This plant, which can surprisingly reach thirty-six feet in height, is a popular addition to many landscapes because of its beautiful purple berries and evergreen, bronze-tinted foliage. Also, the leaves on the California bay-berry are larger than those of its cousins, growing up to four inches in length.

For mid-South gardeners, the wax myrtle (M. *cerifera*) is another large, economy-sized foliage plant, reaching a towering thirty-six-foot height at maturity. It is an evergreen plant producing dense clusters of gray fruit that often remain on the plant throughout the winter; and the twigs, leaves, and fruit are all intensely fragrant.

Most *Myrica* species, even the deciduous ones, have highly aromatic foliage and colorful gray or purple fruits. Because so many varieties of *Myrica* produce prodigious amounts of fragrant, waxy berries, it would seem that any could be pressed into service to provide the wax for a few candles. However, all candle-making directions regarding the bayberry refer specifically to the berries of M. *pensylvanica* (which, for unknown reasons, is also listed in some sources as M. *carolinesis*).

The M. *pensylvanica* is an attractive foliage plant in the garden, and its leaves remain green until they drop in late autumn. The leaves, stems, and flowers are all richly fragrant and can be incorporated into potpourris or sachets when dried; but it is the plant's abundant gray berries, produced in fall, which are valued by candle-makers. If you want to add bayberry candle-making to your family's holiday tradition, I'd recommend you seek out this variety. The American Association of Nurserymen has developed a standard identification code for cultivated plants. For M. *pensylvanica*, the code is MRCPN. Give this code to your garden center when ordering to be sure you obtain the correct species.

Making candles from bayberries is so labor intensive that it was abandoned as a cottage industry in New England as soon as whale oil and paraffin became widely available. Bayberry candles evolved from a necessity into a prized luxury created in late autumn for use during the Christmas holidays and other special occasions or as gifts. They are still wonderfully suited to these purposes and well worth the time it takes to make them. Creating your own aromatic candles is a delightful way to enjoy the spicy scent of your bayberry bushes, and you can smile knowing that you are preserving a truly American way to celebrate a blessed Christmas season.

Deana Deck tends to her flowers, plants, and vegetables at her home in Nashville, Tennessee, where her popular garden column is a regular feature in The Tennessean.

OUR HERITAGE

FROM *THE AUTOBIOGRAPHY* OF BENJAMIN FRANKLIN, 1784

It was about this time that I conceiv'd the bold and arduous Project of arriving at moral Perfection. I wish'd to live without committing any Fault at anytime; I would conquer all that either Natural Inclination, Custom, or Company might lead me into. As I knew, or thought I knew, what was right and wrong, I did not see why I might not *always* do the one and avoid the other. But I soon found I had undertaken a Task of more Difficulty than I had imagined: While my Care was employ'd in guarding against one Fault, I was often surpris'd by another. Habit took the Advantage of Inattention. Inclination was sometimes too strong for Reason. I concluded at length, that the mere speculative Conviction that it was our Interest to be completely virtuous, was not sufficient to prevent our Slipping, and that the contrary Habits must be broken and good Ones acquired and established, before we can have any Dependence on a steady uniform Rectitude of Conduct. For this purpose I therefore contriv'd the following Method. . . .

1. *Temperance.* Eat not to Dulness. Drink not to Elevation.
2. *Silence.* Speak not but what may benefit others or your self. Avoid trifling Conversation.
3. *Order.* Let all your Things have their Places. Let each Part of your Business have its Time.
4. *Resolution.* Resolve to perform what you ought. Perform without fail what you resolve.
5. *Frugality.* Make no Expense but to do good to others or yourself: i.e. Waste nothing.
6. *Industry.* Lose no Time. Be always employ'd in something useful. Cut off all unnecessary Actions.
7. *Sincerity.* Use no hurtful Deceit. Think innocently and justly; and, if you speak; speak accordingly.
8. *Justice.* Wrong none, by doing Injuries or omitting the Benefits that are your Duty.
9. *Moderation.* Avoid Extremes. Forbear resenting Injuries so much as you think they deserve.
10. *Cleanliness.* Tolerate no Uncleanness in Body, Clothes or Habitation.
11. *Tranquility.* Be not disturbed at Trifles, or at Accidents common or unavoidable.
12. *Chastity.* Rarely use Venery but for Health or Offspring; never to Dulness, Weakness, or the Injury of your own or another's Peace or Reputation.
13. *Humility.* Imitate Jesus and Socrates.

ABOUT THE AUTHOR

Although his will began "I, Benjamin Franklin, printer . . .," few men or women have contributed as much to the world as Franklin. Fifteenth of seventeen children, he was born into a poor Boston Puritan household in 1706. He ran away from home and by age seventeen landed in Philadelphia with a job running a printing press. In the years thereafter, he excelled also as inventor (freestanding stove and lightning rod), scientist (acclaimed research on electricity), diplomat (U.S. representative in Paris), writer (Autobiography and Poor Richard's Almanack), revolutionist (helped draft and signed the Declaration of Independence), Deputy Postmaster General for the Colonies (service increased from twice during the winter to once a week), politician (member of the Constitutional Convention), and adviser on moral virtue ("Early to bed and early to rise, makes a man healthy, wealthy, and wise"). Franklin died in 1790 and lies buried beside his wife in the graveyard at Philadelphia's Christ Church.

BENJAMIN FRANKLIN WITH ALEXANDER HAMILTON
Jack Zehrt, artist
FPG International

Christmas Windows

Lon Myruski

Feathery wisps of snowflakes waft
Round haloed streetlamp lights
As church bells of the evening chime
To hail their Yuletide flight.
Down festive, snow-clad, cobbled streets
Come friends and families,
Admiring Christmas windows on
A merry Christmas Eve.

Caroling choirs of children lift
Their voices to extol
The coming of the One who dwells
In faithful hearts and souls.
And in trimmed shops on proud display
He's seen in reverent style—
A crèche in Christmas windows lauds
This little Christmas child.

In homes before a flickering hearth,
Good families gather round
Where warmest Yuletide wishes ring,
Where peace on earth resounds.
And in that glowing firelight,
Eyes gleam in hearts so dear,
Like lustrous Christmas windows filled
With wondrous Christmas cheer.

SIDEWALK SHOPPING
Newcastle, Maine
William Johnson/Johnson's Photography

THROUGH MY WINDOW

Pamela Kennedy

Art by Russ Flint

CHOOSING CHRISTMAS CARDS

With the holiday season on the horizon, it's time again to select Christmas cards. The stores have such a dazzling array of designs, however; it's difficult to choose just the right one. And that's important, because I have a theory about Christmas cards. I believe that people reveal more about themselves than they might think through their holiday greetings. It's not just the message written on the card, but the card itself that says something about who we are.

Reflecting on my own choices of Christmas greetings over the past three decades, I feel qualified to illustrate this little-known phenomenon

with some degree of assurance.

When I was young, unmarried, idealistic, and independent, I searched for the perfect art print. It had to be tasteful, subtle, and reproduced on very heavy stock. I carefully coordinated my shade of ink with that of the printing on the card and wrote deep, meaningful messages in flawless longhand. I wanted my Christmas cards to make a statement beyond the words on the paper.

As a new bride endeavoring to be sensitive to my husband, I suggested he have some input in the Christmas card selection process. In the department store near our home, I gently directed him toward the snowy European scenes in subdued hues. I quickly learned the meaning of opposites attracting! Subtlety went out the window as he gravitated toward the largest cards in the rack and then looked for the ones with the most gold foil. He apparently came from the "bigger is better" school of Christmas greetings.

After some tense times, we settled on an art print on medium stock with a gold foil border. The next year I suggested he check out the holiday sales in the tool department while I took on the chore of choosing cards. He seemed delighted.

A few years into my married life, I hit my creative period and cast off the mantle of materialistic, mass-produced Christmas cards in favor of original poetry reproduced on parchment. I was giving myself as a gift, I mused.

Then there was the year I was consumed with concerns about the shallowness of society and sent out cards bearing thinly veiled political messages decrying the loss of the true spirit of Christmas. Surprisingly, my friends and family didn't take my Christmas accusations personally. I eventually realized that my self-righteous zeal had only proved the point of the message on my cards! The next year, I found lovely ones expressing gratitude for good friends and sent them out as a personal act of atonement.

While still believing my Christmas greetings involved sending a bit of myself, after the arrival of our first child, I felt I had precious little of myself left to send. Moving past my philosophical phase, I passed up poetry and politics for manger scenes with chubby infants and winsome Madonnas. I suspect my taste in cards might have had something to do with all those happy babies, not one of whom seemed to be suffering from colic, gas, or diaper rash. And that serene Mary! What I wouldn't give for a fraction of her peacefulness!

In the years before we had children, I couldn't understand why people sent rambling, endless chronicles of their family activities. I really didn't care how many soccer goals little Jennifer made or how Mark's project got rave reviews at the science fair. Of course all that changed once we had progeny of our own. It was challenging to fit all their wondrous accomplishments on a single sheet of paper, and I spent hours composing just the right message to send—something between bare facts and blatant boasting.

As our creative and brilliant offspring hit adolescence, I found I could squeeze their amazing accomplishments nicely into a half page. Many things were left unsaid. After all, our darlings might suddenly snap out of their current obnoxious stage; then I'd have to send retractions to everyone on our Christmas list! During those years, financial concerns impacted our Christmas card choices too. With college tuition looming, braces blooming, and everyone growing at phenomenal rates, I found I could save a bundle on Christmas cards by purchasing them a year ahead at the after-holiday sales. During that period, my tastes in illustration leaned toward those designs that still remained in sufficient quantity to meet my needs.

I've passed into a new phase in the last few years. I'm much more relaxed about Christmas cards now. I like cards with a simple, meaningful message, and I enjoy typing a short note to include in each. When I send the card, I imagine tucking in a prayer and a hug as well. Many of our friends live far away; and with our busy lives and theirs, we often only communicate at Christmas.

This year, as usual, I look forward to catching up on all the news from distant friends and relatives. I will no doubt receive a wide selection of art prints, large foil cards, newsy family-grams, photos, and even a political statement or two. It doesn't matter. Each one gives me a little glimpse of the person sending it and says more than what is written in the card. It reminds me I have a wonderful array of friends and family, all at different ages and stages of life, each one precious and thoughtful enough to wish me well at Christmastime.

Pamela Kennedy is a freelance writer of short stories, articles, essays, and children's books. Wife of a naval officer and mother of three children, she has made her home on both U.S. coasts and currently resides in Honolulu, Hawaii. She draws her material from her own experiences and memories, adding highlights from her imagination to enhance the story.

Christmas Card
Edith G. Schay

You sent a pine sprig with your card;
And right beyond my sunny yard
I see the North, far hills, tall pines,
Warm wishes from your hearth to mine.

Oh, tell me, did you really know
You sent me silver-scented snow,
Sent memories touched with tinsel-shine,
Sent Christmas in one sprig of pine?

Just an Old Card
Phyllis C. Michael

Just look at this! It's quite a list!
I wonder, would one card be missed?
I surely can't take time to write
To all these folks! Besides, they might
Not ever think of me again;
At least that's how it's always been.
I think I'll send no more than six;
Then I'll have much more time to fix
Some decorations and a tree
That's really beautiful to see.
I just can't rush around, I say;
And what's an old card anyway?

Oh, there's the mailman! Let me see.
Why here's a card from Madge to me!
She says she often thinks of days
When we both rode in one-horse sleighs.
Ah, yes, I too remember how;
But that, all that, is long gone now.

And here's a card from Cousin Nell!
She says they're lonely, but all is well.
I haven't written once this year—
I should have though; she's such a dear.
And look at this card all in gold,
Expressing words the angels told.
Ann says she hopes I'm truly blessed
With all that makes me happiest.

And who's this card from? Well, just look!
It's Sue! I see she even took
The time to say she baked a cake
Just like my mother used to make
At Christmastime! Well, bless her heart!
I guess it's time I got a start!
Now where's my pen and all those stamps?
I'm going to turn up all the lamps;
'Cause I have quite a lengthy list,
And not one person shall be missed.

Colors of Christmas

Nora M. Bozeman

Reds and yellows, blues and greens—
Christmas paints her Yuletide scenes.
Brilliant cards in colors bold,
Ornaments of red and gold,

Festive stores and scenery,
Frosty panes in filigree,
Trees ashine in silvered snow,
Star-strung avenues aglow,

Winter white and cheeks of red,
Sapphire skies hung overhead,
Hanging swags of evergreens
Color all my Christmas scenes.

POINSETTIAS
Gene Ahrens Photography

Christmas Spirit

Nick Kenny

Something happens in December,
Something strange beyond our ken.
All the world becomes so friendly;
Kindness seems to bloom again.

Children act like little angels;
Grownups' tempers all are furled.
Such transitions make you wonder
If you're in another world.

What a shame this Christmas spirit
With its friendliness and cheer
Disappears with each December;
It should really last all year!

If I Were a Christmas Tree

Bonnie Compton Hanson

I'd like to be a Christmas tree
    With presents all around,
With golden ropes and silver tinsel
    Hanging to the ground.
I'd trim my boughs with crystal balls
    Of red and blue and white
And watch them glow and catch the gleam
    Of every Christmas light.
I'd wrap myself in candy canes
    And popcorn balls and such;
And last, I'd have a shining angel
    For my crowning touch!
Then early Christmas morn when little ones
    With shouts of joy
Rushed in to see and claim and treasure
    Every wondrous toy,
I'd lean my boughs to brush up close
    And touch each child like this
And place upon each sleepy cheek
    My loving Christmas kiss!

The Christmas Light

John C. Bonser

I love the sight of Christmas lights
This season of the year
And merry sounds that now abound
In melodies of cheer!

I love the words that may be heard
In carols that are sung,
The happy cries and sparkling eyes
Among the very young!

I love the scenes of evergreens
And wreaths hung everywhere,
Soft, falling snow and candle-glow
And people bowed in prayer!

I love the bells whose message tells
The sweetest story told,
How goodness still our lives can fill
As God's great plan unfolds!

I love the light, that special night,
The shepherds saw afar
And ran to find for humankind—
His bright and morning star!

Readers' Forum

Meet Our Ideals Readers and Their Families

The editors at Ideals magazine are always looking for well-written, nostalgic reminiscences. If you have a particular memory that takes us back to the treasured days of yesteryear, send your typed manuscript to: NOSTALGIC REMINISCENCES, C/O EDITORIAL DEPARTMENT, IDEALS MAGAZINE, P.O. BOX 305300, NASHVILLE, TENNESSEE 37230.

GINA LORETI of Solebury, Pennsylvania, shares with us this picture of her son, Brandon, age three and a half, showing his overflowing Christmas spirit, complete with half-eaten candy cane. Gina has been a faithful *Ideals* fan for ten years; and she, her husband, Danny, and Brandon love sharing *Ideals* as they drive to and from nearby New York City and Philadelphia to visit family and friends. Gina also enjoys sharing the pictures and poems with her kindergarten students.

From MARGIE NEAL comes this photograph of grandchildren Jared Neal (age three) and Matt Barber (age one). The boys were visiting Margie and her husband Walter at their farm in Durand, Michigan, the site of last year's family gathering during the Christmas season. The wicker basket, the perfect size for young Matt, is Margie's own handiwork. Walter says, "She's good at everything she puts her hands to." Thanks for sharing, Margie and Walter—and merry Christmas to the family!

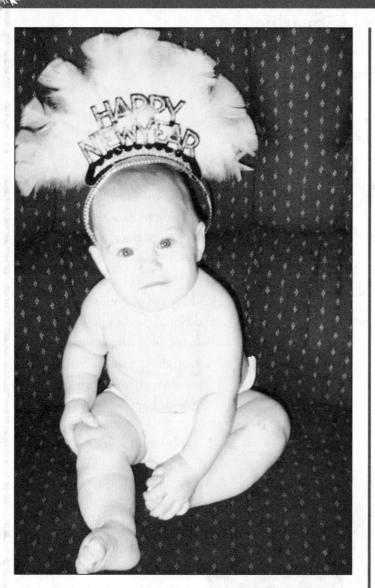

TAMI BURKHART, who lives in Bucyrus, Ohio, sent us this picture of her granddaughter, Kendra Kay Hudson, doing her best impression of Baby New Year. Kendra loves to play dress up with "Grammie"; and Tami says that Kendra is very photogenic and loves to pose for the camera, so snapping this shot just added to the fun. Kendra, now fourteen months old, is the daughter of Craig and Karen Hudson.

THANK YOU Gina Loreti, Margie Neal, and Tami Burkhart for sharing with *Ideals*. We hope to hear from other readers who would like to share photos and stories with the Ideals family. Please include a self-addressed, stamped envelope if you would like the photos returned. Keep your original photographs for safekeeping and send duplicate photos along with your name, address, and telephone number to:

READERS' FORUM
IDEALS PUBLICATIONS INC.
P.O. BOX 305300
NASHVILLE, TENNESSEE 37230

ideals®

Publisher, Patricia A. Pingry
Editor, Lisa C. Ragan
Copy Editor, Michelle Prater Burke
Electronic Prepress, Anne Lesemann
Editorial Assistant, Brian L. Bacon
Editorial Intern, Connie L. Flood
Contributing Editors,
Lansing Christman, Deana Deck, Russ Flint,
Pamela Kennedy, Patrick McRae, Mary
Skarmeas, Nancy Skarmeas

ACKNOWLEDGMENTS

WHEN MARY . . . by Rachel Field reprinted with the permission of Simon & Schuster Books for Young Readers from *POEMS* by Rachel Field. Copyright © 1941 Macmillan Publishing Company; copyright renewed © 1969 Arthur S. Pederson. FIRST CHRISTMAS EVE from *LIVING THE YEARS* by Edgar A. Guest, copyright © 1949 by The Reilly & Lee Co. Used with permission of the author's estate. CHRISTMAS VISITOR by Edgar Daniel Kramer. Reprinted by permission of the author's estate. STAR AND SONG from *THE SHINING THREAD* by Jessie Wilmore Murton. Reprinted by permission of Pacific Press Publishing Association. Our sincere thanks to the following author whom we were unable to contact: Vic Jameson for THREE GIFTS.

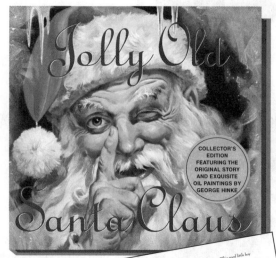